HANDTALK

AN ABC OF FINGER SPELLING & SIGN LANGUAGE

REMY CHARLIP   MARY BETH   GEORGE ANCONA

PUBLISHED BY FOUR WINDS PRESS   NEW YORK, NEW YORK

Library of Congress Cataloging in Publication Data

Charlip, Remy.
　Handtalk.

　Reprint of the ed. published by Parents' Magazine Press, New
York.
　SUMMARY: An introduction to two kinds of sign language: finger
spelling, or forming words letter by letter with the fingers, and
signing, or making signs with one or two hands for each word or
idea.
　1. Sign language — Juvenile literature. [1. Sign language. 2.
Alphabet] I. Mary Beth, joint author. II. Ancona, George. III. Title.
[P117.C5 1980]　　　　　419　　　　　80-16750
ISBN 0-590-07766-X

Published by Four Winds Press
A division of Scholastic Magazines, Inc., New York, N.Y.
Text copyright © 1974 by Remy Charlip and Mary Beth Miller
Illustrations copyright © 1974 by Remy Charlip
Photographs copyright © 1974 by George Ancona
All rights reserved
Printed in the United States of America
Library of Congress Catalog Card Number: 80-16750
1　2　3　4　5　84　83　82　81　80

FOR MY FATHER CHESTER, MY MOTHER NELLIE, MY SISTER BEVERLY

A

ANGEL

B U G

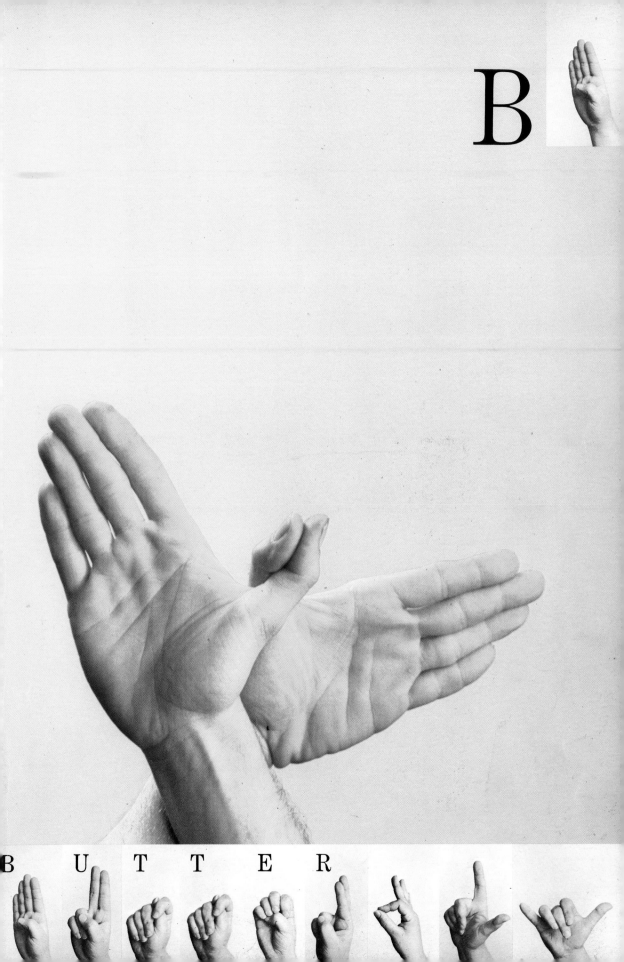

B

B U T T E R

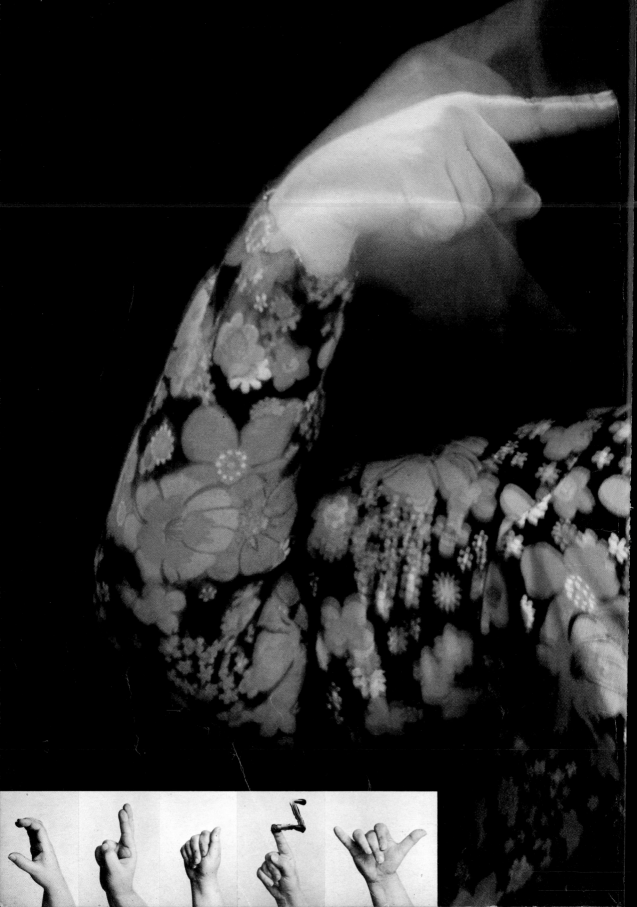

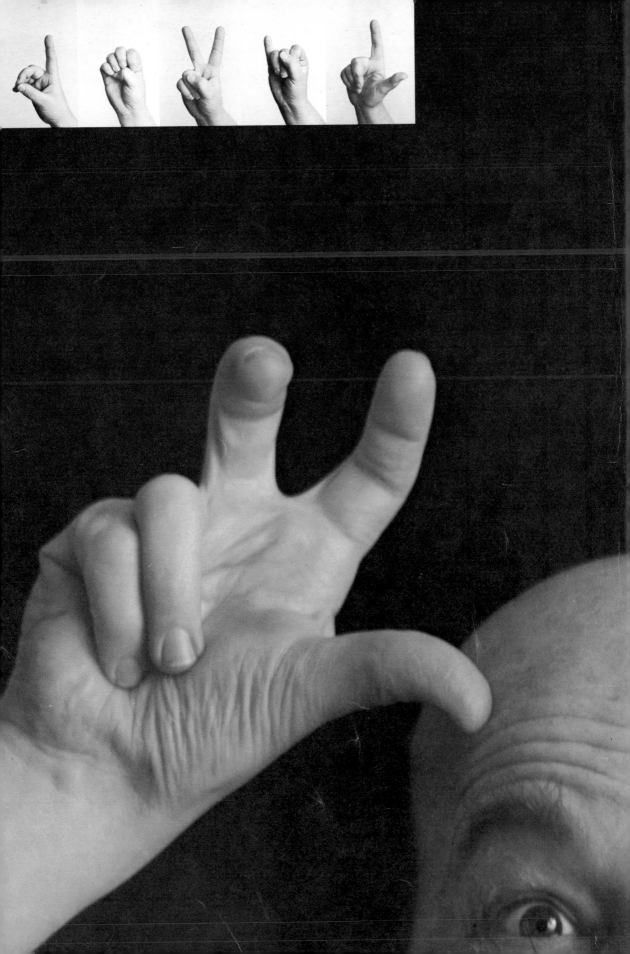

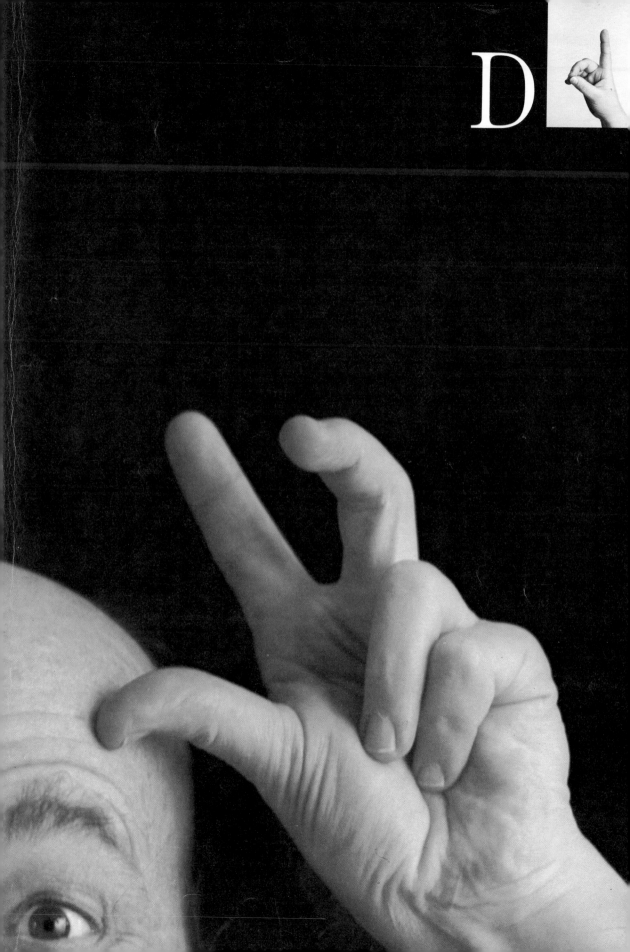

D

E

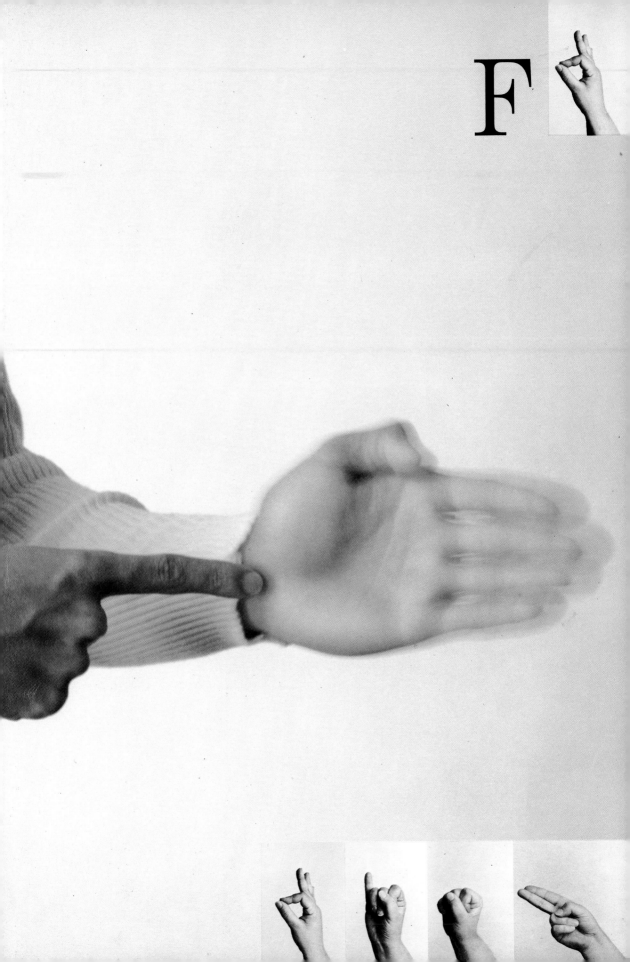

F

G

H

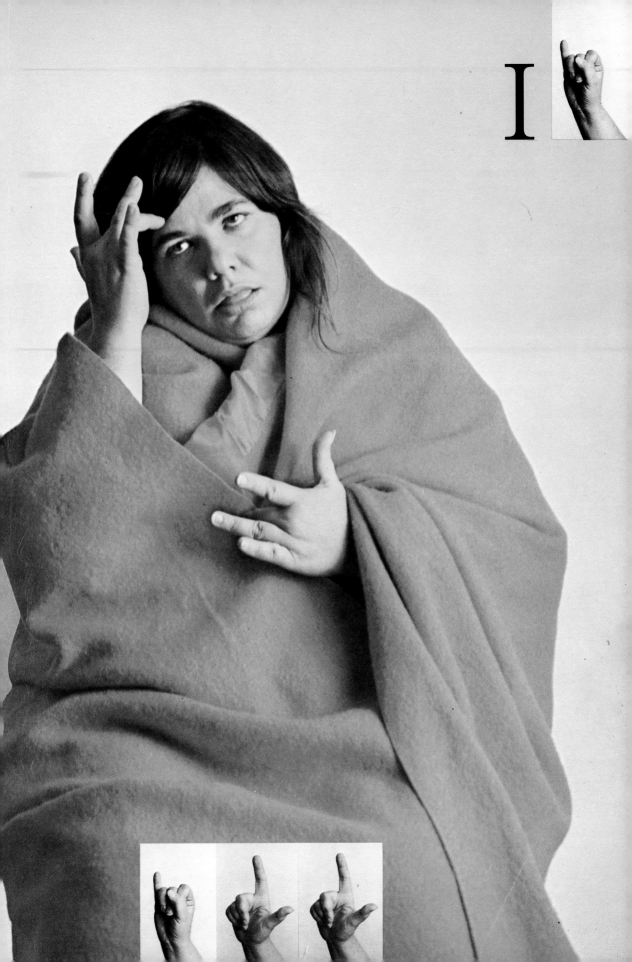

I

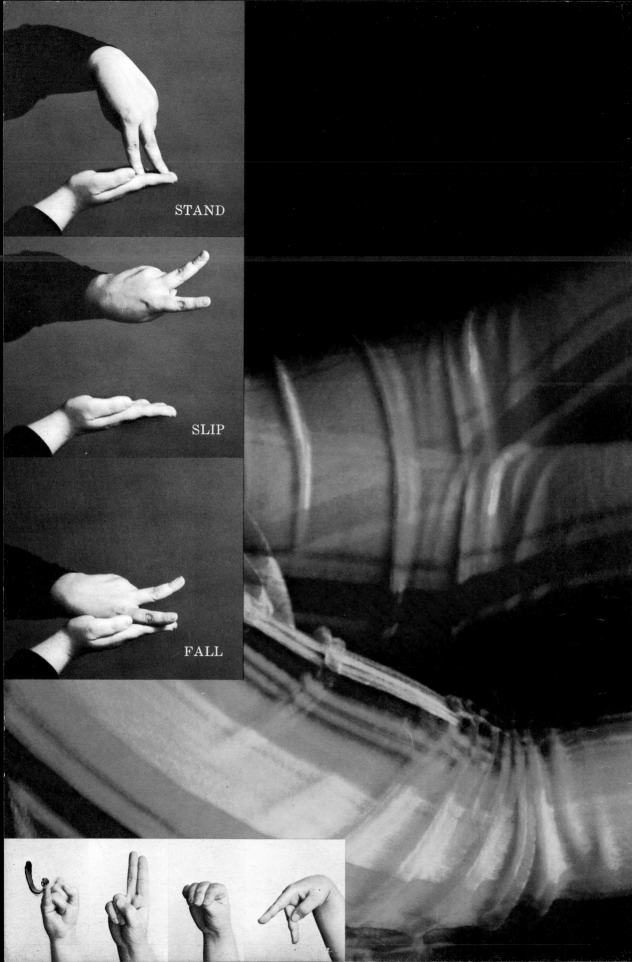

STAND

SLIP

FALL

J

TWO FINGERS STAND, THEN GO UP, AND LAND AGAIN

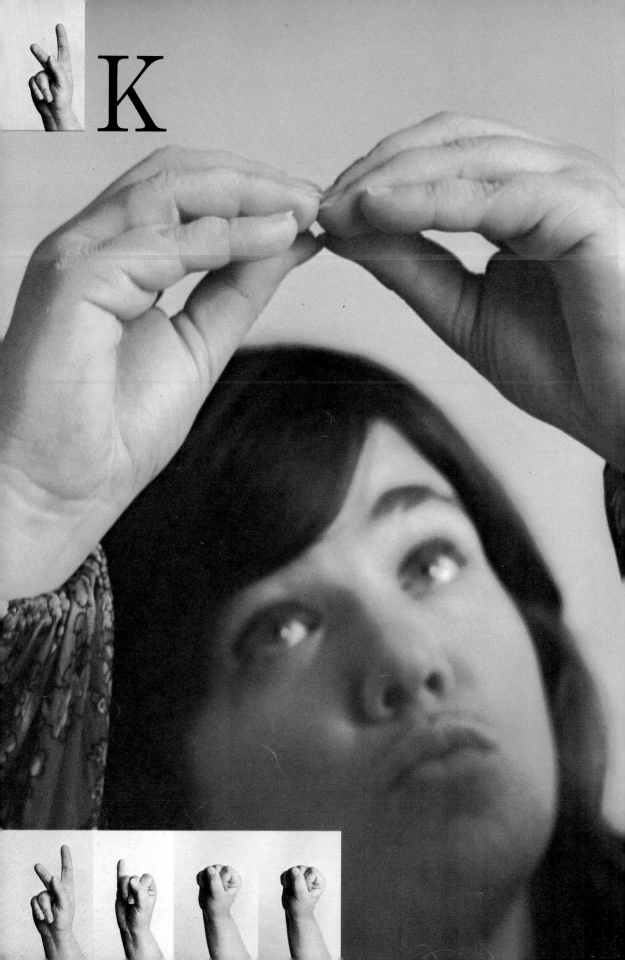

K

L

M

820067

N

TAP THE TIPS OF THE 3 FINGERS YOU USE TO MAKE

NO   NO   NO

O

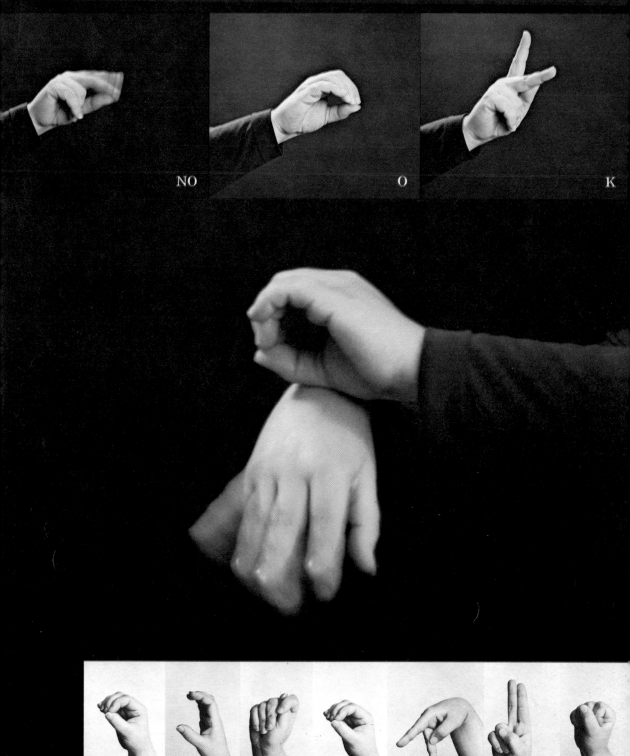

NO   O   K

PEANUT   BUTTER

WHEN YOU CLOSE THESE PAGES   THESE

P

AND

JELLY

HANDS   MAKE THE SIGN FOR SANDWICH

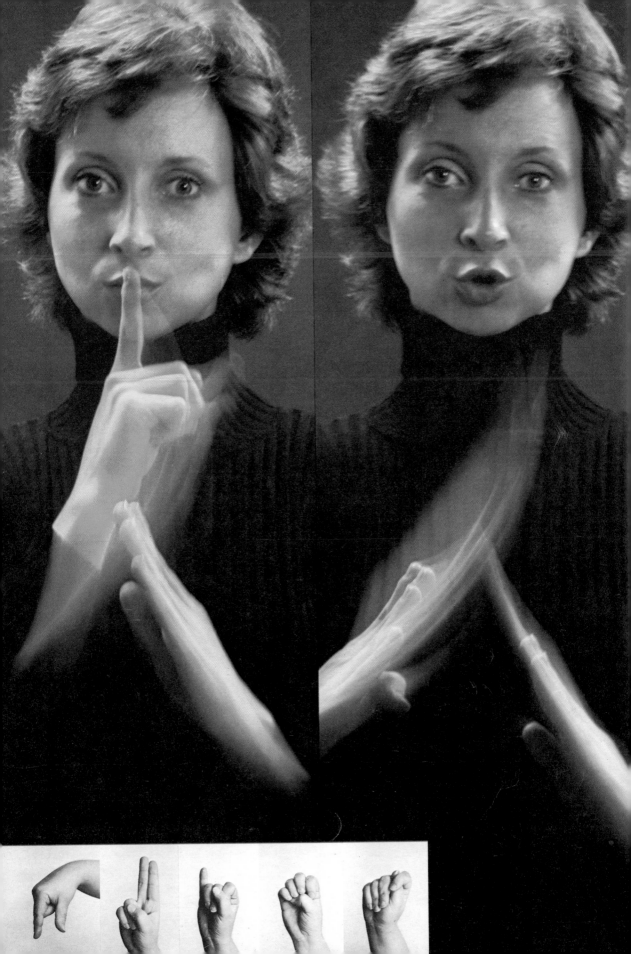

R

S

CIRCLE WITH FINGER, THEN OPEN SAME HAND

T

YOU CAN WIGGLE ITS HEAD

U

V

IN........ A VERY............... UGLY............... VILLAGE...........

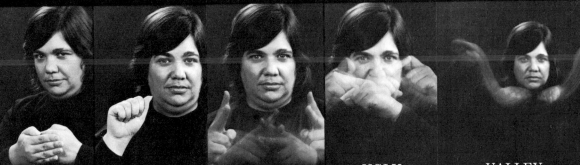

.....NEAR...... A VERY............... UGLY............... VALLEY......

UNDER........ A VERY.............. UGLY VOLCANO...........

.....LIVED........ A VERY............ UGLY............... VAMPIRE...........

WITH HIS BEAUTIFUL VULTURE

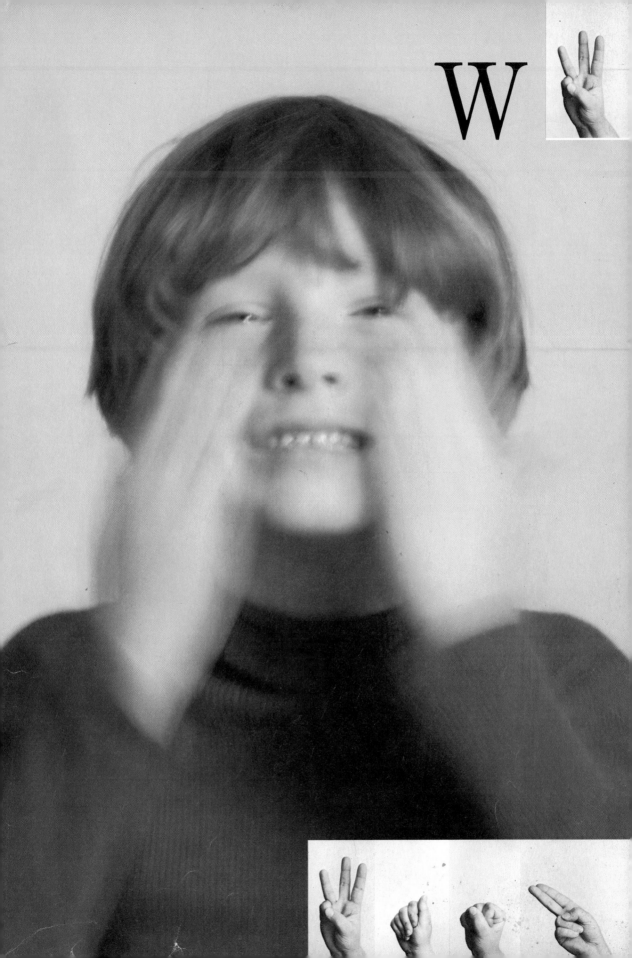

W

OPEN AND CLOSE THE FINGERS OF ONE HAND LIKE THE SHUTTER
OF A CAMERA. IT IS ALSO THE SIGN FOR A FLASH OF LIGHT.

X

COMBINE 3 LETTERS FOR SHORTHAND: I LOVE YOU

Y

Z

COOK	DEAD	EGG
ICE CREAM	JOIN	KITE
OWL	PUSH	QUICK
UPSET	VALENTINE	WITH